FYLATOS PUBLISHING

Publish on Demand, Inc.
© Fylatos Publishing,
Delaware 2018

Author: Maria Vitoratos

© Fylatos Publishing, Maria Vitoratos
e-mail: contact@fylatos.com
web: www.fylatos.com

Pagination-Design: © Fylatos Publishing
ISBN: 978-618-5318-47-5

EMPOWERMENT

For Teens

A Guide to Helping Young Adults
Prepare for Their Future

Maria Vitoratos

Fylatos Publishing
Delaware
MMXVIII

This book is dedicated to teenagers near and far.
The world will be a better place because of them.

Contents

Introduction

The idea for this book came to me one day months after my friend and colleague, Adam, told me that I should consider creating a book that could capture my work and bring it to schools around the world. At that time, I thought it sounded like a good idea, but I was not sure how I could possibly write anything about coaching that had not already been written. I parked the idea for months and unconsciously carried it with me. If I am being honest, it actually felt like I forgot all about it until one Thursday afternoon, when the first title for this book suddenly came to me. Again, it happened during another conversation with Adam when I was telling him about my professional plans, and then I told him that I would write the book. He was thrilled and asked what the title of the book would be.

'From the boardroom to the classroom,' I declared. I did not even think about it, I just blurted it out!

His response was, 'You mean, from the classroom to the boardroom?'

'No,' I said, very confidently. 'It is going to be a book that shares my secrets of bringing the boardroom into the classroom.'

Fast-forward a few weeks after my last conversation with Adam, and I was sitting on a plane, bound for a journey of self-reflection in Greece with the intent that this book would be born along the way. Typically, when I have a creative idea, they have a great conception, but life gets the best of me and I do not finish them. *This time will be different,* I promised myself. *I believe passionately in the work, so, if not now... when?*

I wholeheartedly hope you enjoy every tip, skill, and thought-provoking idea that will be shared within this book. The experiences that are being shared with you have been an accumulation of the work that I have been doing for over eight years. This is not just a job for me; I believe that this is my purpose and anyone who has seen me in action will say I am extremely motivated and enthusiastic, but also a little bit of a mad scientist.

Alas, the time has come to turn the page and enjoy the journey that lies ahead. May this book inspire you to empower teenagers wherever you are in the world. Every teenager that we inspire can only add greater hope for an empowered group of future leaders in our world. This work is not for the fainthearted. This is the work of bold and audacious educators who want to plough through the teenage myth and continue to pursue this journey of teenage empowerment. Have fun with it because fun is at the heart of this work!

Exciting days ahead!

—Maria Vitoratos

CHAPTER ONE

What is the Dream?

Whenever a student walks into my office for the first time, I always start with the same question: 'How can I help you today?' Usually, they will tell me that they do not know what course to take or what they should do after they complete their university studies. For many, they rarely make eye contact.

Apologies and concerns for not knowing all the answers is also a common reaction at the start of this discussion. I will always give them enough time during this first session to share their academic journey with me for the first few minutes. Doing this helps them share their past experiences and it gives me a starting point for our conversation and our work together.

The art of listening to their responses is key at this stage. I rarely interrupt them and will only ask them how they made their choices. It is important that I understand their thought process along their journey. Most teenagers have never had a talk with their guardian or pastoral teacher that allowed them enough time to discuss their choices without being interrupted.

Using my experience with teenagers, this first session will define how I create a sense of trust in my service and how to develop rapport to connect with them. The teen will either walk away from my office feeling heard and they will return for another session or they will walk away potentially feeling judged, never to return. The latter is never my aim nor my hope for any student who signs up for a session with me. If I can get them through my door voluntarily, I want to ensure that they keep coming back.

THEIR STORY IS WHERE IT ALL BEGINS

Once the student has told me about their academic experiences, I invite them on a journey into their future. At the start of this exercise, it is a struggle for most of my young clients. Teenagers today are not given the opportunity to dream about the future. Studies, exams, and extracurricular activities are eating up their time and none of these responsibilities allow them the time to dream about the possibilities that lay ahead for them. How do we encourage our students to empower their career choices if we rarely give them time to dream them up? This first session allows time for the student to reflect on what their biggest dreams are. What would they like to achieve if they could choose the outcome of their life? Responses such as cars, houses, traveling, and money are always common and as a rule of thumb, I never pass judgement or shun them.

Once the student can share their dreams, the magic begins to unravel. For most, however, they do not know what to say and often ask me for more clarification. 'What do you mean, Maria? Can you give me an example?' High school students today seem to need many reassurances that they are going to get the right answer before they even try. A coaching session that involves dreaming expects that the student can dream it up. There are no right answers. There are no standards of acceptable dreams. I often spend more time normalizing this fact with my coachees during these sessions because it is important. By the time a student is sitting in my office, they may have undergone about 12 years of being told that they must study to get the answers right on the test. It is important to let them know that although their years of education have taught them there is a right or wrong answer, dreaming does not follow this pattern.

They will be skeptical; after all, wouldn't we all be skeptical if we were fed the same secret to success for over twelve consecutive years and then suddenly, some life coach tells us that life does not always need the right answer? How would you feel comfortable dreaming up confidently after hearing that? Feel compassion for your young client; they need time and they will begin to try only when they are ready. Are you ready? Have you tried discovering your dreams? Unless you have, you cannot confidently or authentically do this exercise with the student sitting in your office. I never preach unless I have first practiced what I am preaching. I know the red flags and I will share them with my client but first, I must help them cross over the edge of fear and start to dream.

Dreaming is underrated. In our society, the average academic institution does not dedicate curriculum time to it and it is not presently identified as a factor of importance for a student's academic journey. However, in my opinion, it is the secret to success for any empowered person. The dream is the starting point. The vision comes from the dream. The dream is also the fuel that keeps us strong during challenging times or in times of distress. The dream is the hope and the key to persistence that drives our resilience. Dream big or go home, is what I always say. Why would I dream small if I can dream big? What are we afraid of?

If we study the history of education, we can see that at every stage of humanity, education served a different purpose. From children using play as a method of self-teaching during the hunting and gathering stages to the present day, different key social players from village rulers to religious leaders and politicians all had their thumb on the education system.

I do believe that overall, education as an institution is a central entity that socializes our future leaders for the working world and to maintain society. I am a firm believer in the power of education and I honor the system for its intentions. However, I also believe that the education system should not be a static entity; it is dynamic and must change and develop at the same pace as technology. As members of society, we are required to pass the torch to our future leaders and where best to teach them all the necessary skills than at school?

Unfortunately, as it stands in most parts of the world, schools are feeding students test materials and grade phobia. Students today are not encouraged by society to be dreamers and creators of their own future. Tertiary education still forces the highest grade-earners to have access to the best programs around the world and students are expected to maintain the highest grades to even be considered for these university courses. Making matters worse, students are losing grand opportunities not because of a lack of intelligence but only because they were either too immature to stay focused on their studies or because they were unable to master the art of memorizing data for exams. Additionally, sometimes they are simply not inspired to learn because the subject matter just did not align with their interests.

Sessions with a Careers Coach allows the student time to dream it up. Do not allow them to escape this stage of the session because they are afraid of getting it wrong. Dreaming is not something that we should take for granted and it is NOT a waste of time. Every successful person in the history of human nature had a dream. The dream is the starting point and if we cannot dream when we are young, when will we have time to dream?

When the student can creatively share their dreams for the future, your job as a coach in this session is almost complete. Did you cheerlead them through the session? Bring out the rah-rahs and shout aloud for them! They need to feel alive and they need you to get excited with them. I believe that the most vital role of a coach, teacher, guardian, or parent is to show support and the support must be positive. Who are we to dismiss their dreams? It is vital that we do not allow our limiting beliefs to dim their spark. Dreaming is an edgy experience and feeling supported along the journey is very important.

When the cheers are celebrated, the plenary part of the session has begun. It consists of asking the young coachee what they learned about themselves during this dreaming phase. Ask them to spend the next few minutes reflecting on their dreams. How do they feel about sharing the dream with another person? Do they believe that the dream is ready for the world and worthy of sharing, or do they wish to keep it hidden from the world? I tend to give them a couple of minutes to think about their self-learning before they share it with me. The practice of self-reflection is usually the opportunity for the greatest recognition of achievement for students in any area of their lives, but most especially, it is a necessary element of their learning at the end of a coaching session. Do not walk over it and never end the session without it.

Their answers to the questions that I encourage you to ask at this stage will give you another very important insight into their minds. Their confidence and conviction in their dreams becomes very apparent at this stage. Ask them to expand on why they do or do not believe the dream is possible. Why is it worthy of sharing? And if it is not worthy, why would that be? This discussion should take up the remainder of the session. Never end the dreaming session abruptly; the teen needs ample time to self-reflect on their key learnings.

Finally, congratulate them and continue giving them some more cheers for their fabulous work during the session. Keep them excited as they walk away; ensure that they remember their moments with you as ones that lifted them higher than any past experience with an educator ever could. Doing this will plant feelings of 'wow' in their memory. You want the 'wow', because this feeling will bring them back. It always does. 'Wow' is an addictive feeling. 'Wow' is where dreams live strong and have the potential to come alive.

When the student leaves my office, I always keep notes of everything we discussed. Note-taking ensures that I will remember what we did, and I can prepare for our next session. Note-taking also shows the student that their words are important and worthy of being remembered. Show them that you remember their words in the next session by recapping what was discussed before you move on to a new topic.

ALL-TIME FAVOURITE DREAMING QUESTIONS

1. What could you achieve in your life if you took the time to dream it up?

2. If money and time would never be an issue, what could you achieve?

3. When you were a young child, what did you want to be when you grew up?

4. What is a dream life for you?

5. If there was a dream hidden deep within you, what would it be?

6. If you believed that dreams do come true, what could your life become?

SUMMARY OF THE DREAMING STAGE:

✓ Build rapport with your student/client/child.

✓ Let them share their academic journey and discuss their decision-making process.

✓ Invite them (never force them!) to travel with you on a journey into the future and ask them to dream it up with you aloud. *(Some students may need time to reflect before they share this with you. Offer them a sheet of paper to write down their dream/vision before they share it with you.)*

✓ Cheerlead, cheerlead, cheerlead! Bring out the pom-poms and get excited for them! Their dream is coming to life and it is an amazing experience. Look excited and sound excited. They will stay motivated if they see you bringing their dream to life.

✓ Give the student/client/child time to self-reflect on their learnings from the session. What did they discover in the last 50 minutes that they did not already know when they arrived for the session?

✓ Keep clear notes that will help you pick up where you left off in the next session. Keep your notes concise and easy to understand.

Chapter Two

What is Your Gift?

When a student returns for the second session, we recap what was discussed in our previous session. This revisit allows us to rediscover the dream and it allows me to cheerlead some more. Continue building rapport; continue building a great working relationship with your young client. It is important that you tap back into the feeling of 'wow' with them. The 'wow' is what they will remember most from their last session. Bring them back to that feeling and from there, start asking them some very big reflection questions.

I always begin the session in the same manner every time they return. This routine allows the teen to feel like they know what to expect from my sessions. This is a very comforting feeling for our slightly anxious young adults. I do tend to add a sparkle of change in small bits but overall, I keep most elements of my sessions as predictable as possible. For many reading this, you may feel like a Life Coach should never have routines, but in my experience, the routine of certain parts of the session keeps the client feeling safe and mostly, they feel a sense of knowing what to expect. I believe that this allows them to relax and feel comfortable knowing that not everything will be uncomfortable, and they can relax with you as their coach.

In this session, unless the student has requested to use their time with me on something specific, I will request that we discuss 'their gift'. The most obvious comment from my young clients is always, 'What is a gift? What do you mean? Like something I buy or receive?' I never give the answer away. In true coaching style, I will ask them about famous or successful people whom they are familiar with and ask them what they think their gifts were or are.

For example, Steve Jobs is a common successful role model. His gift, according to most students, was that he had a great eye for technology. The conversation continues with me asking them to identify the benefits that Steve received because of his gift. We then move onto asking them to identify what the benefits were for the world, because Steve Jobs shared his gift. The idea behind this exercise is to show teenagers that when something great exists within us and we share it, the entire world can also benefit.

Just as with the 'Dreaming Session', this session will require that the student is able to get past the idea of getting the right answer. Remember, there are no right answers, everyone is different, and everyone will have a different gift.

THE NEED TO SUCCEED

As within the education system, most teenagers are on the journey to succeed—and by succeed, I mean to be the best and make the most money or have the greatest recognition possible. The bigger, the better.

Although this sounds like teens aiming high, I have seen that teens are also aiming blind. They do not seem to know what they are aiming for. Is it a material reward or is it their life's purpose?

Somewhere along the way, the grades and the academic recognition that they have received has not taught them that in life outside the gates of school, success is not objective, and it is not very clear-cut. Not all the straight-A students are successful, and they certainly do not make the most money. Life is subjective and most definitely depends on perspective, resilience, and persistence. Most importantly, what we have learned from the successful individuals of the world is that life outside the school gates is like a climbing a mountain. There are no smooth ridges; it is always up, down, and all around.

Doubt, fear, and challenge are all common recipes for life after graduation. For some, the scars that they earned from their sharp ridges have become a story of their success. For others, the falls and the fails are the recipes for resilience.

Students of all ages—but for the sake of this book, teenagers—must understand while they are still in school that life is filled with critics and doubters. Life is a journey and the journey will not always have opportunities for a do-over; there are certainly no dress rehearsals. Every day, it is the real deal. This is all part of the learning experience we call LIFE.

As parents and educators, we must offer our teens more practical opportunities to allow them to be prepared for the critics and doubters in the real world. We must help them practice using their wings. Will they land on their feet? Will they fall and struggle to get back up again? Will they find the strength to continue climbing their mountains? We must prepare them and teach them that the world needs them to climb those mountains. There will always be a struggle. Regardless of what path our teens will decide to take, there will always be a struggle. The million-dollar question is: Will they have the skills to survive the path they take?

THE PATH OF YOUR GIFT OR THE PATH OF REGRET

I thoroughly enjoy reading self-development books and articles that feed my coaching mind. I listen to empowering talks and quench my thirst for empowerment by practicing empowerment tools that help me do better and be better. I always bring back my greatest learnings to my sessions. I believe that the best teachers and coaches are always the ones who learn and bring the learning to their lessons and sessions. The focus for this second session was inspired by the numerous empowerment talks and books that have given me a new perspective on my life and my work.

Just as I request of my young clients in the first session, I also took the time to discover my gift. This next session demonstrates how I have been able to help my clients identify theirs.

I always tell the students that everyone has a gift, but not everyone will recognize what those gifts are. For some, their gift is the way they can make someone feel empowered; for others, it is a skill they have that enriches someone else's life. Everyone has a gift and everyone's gift is needed and important in this world. Your gift is not an entitlement based on gender, culture, religion, or education. It is a gift that everyone is born with. I like to call it your 'human-print'. It is that something special or unique that you do well, and you do it unconsciously and ever so naturally.

In this session—just as in the dreaming session—our time is used to help the student identify what their gift is. It is important to remember that every session always feeds into the next. There are never isolated sessions in my coaching practice. This is another reason why note-taking—as mentioned in the previous chapter—is very important. The ability to transfer information from one session to another is very important for the progression of the student's coaching program.

Since I was a teacher in my past career, I use the lesson plan structure in all my coaching sessions. The introduction is my opportunity to normalize discussing their gift. We discuss it regardless of what path they choose to take in their life, be it the one that their journey through academia has dictated or the one that follows the beat of their heart.

There will always be times of struggle and pain. On the one hand, the pain and struggle may come from the challenging road less travelled or the struggle may come from the pain of regret for not taking it. Either way, LIFE was created for the brave and for the living. There is no escaping the struggles of life. The prerequisite for living is in handling the doubters and critics. It is about overcoming challenge and surfing the waves, no matter how scary they may seem.

Many times, the critics and doubters are not on the outside; they live within us and in fact, we become our own worst critics and doubters.

At this stage in our session, I spend a good amount of time educating the teen in my office. To some, it sounds like a preaching session, but I call it the 'theory aspect' of their coaching session. We discuss the roads and paths of life and we discuss the potential challenges and pain that may exist for them. We discuss their parents' journey and what they would have done differently if they could have a do-over. We discuss some of their role models. These are the people whom my clients feel are the model of success. We discuss and try to identify what they believe their gifts are. We discuss what life would be like if their role models did not use their gifts.

In a nutshell, before I encourage the student to identify their own gifts, I sell the benefits of the gifts that exist in the people they look up to. My coaching badge may say 'coach' but I spend a lot of time normalizing, educating, and selling ideas and theories to my young clients. The client buy-in is a measure of success for every session; if they believe that coaching can help them, they will be open to trying.

Taking the time to do these things is another opportunity to continue building great rapport with them. They realize and become comfortable when they know that I am not pushing their journey through change; I am empowering them with knowledge and information that they can use.

THE GIFT FEEDS THE DREAM

Using my effective DG questions, I can help the student begin to identify their gift and continue to clearly identify the benefits of achieving their dream life. The DG questions are asked in a specific order that ensures self-discovery, but they are also essential in helping the coach take the student through the necessary stages that lead them to identify their gift.

THE DG LIST OF QUESTIONS:

1. What is your dream life? What does it look like? What does it feel like to be living this life?

2. What skills do you think you need to live the life that you described above?

3. What characteristics will you need to adopt (if you do not already have them) to live the life that you described above?

4. What have you learned in your life already that will be a benefit or required skill in the life that you described above?

5. What else already exists within you that you know will be needed in the life that you described above?

6. Let's recap your dream life again. What does it look like? What does it feel like to be living this life? What kind of people will you be surrounded by in this life?

7. Who is your biggest fan? Name someone that will cheer for you the loudest. What would that person say that you do well and would be a valuable skill or characteristic in the life that you described above?

8. Now, I want you to think about a pattern of positive comments that teachers from your past have all said about you. What is the most common comment?

9. What do you do so well without even trying that you never really give much attention to?

For some students, the list of questions above will allow them to dig into their skills or behavior traits, which will enable them to notice something about themselves that makes them unique. For others, it may trigger them into feeling like they do not have the skills or traits required for their dream life. As an experienced coach, you must be prepared for either scenario. If the latter shows up, normalize, normalize, normalize. Feelings of inability or impossibility are not uncommon for people of every age group but most especially for teenagers. It is very unfortunate that our students spend so much time studying and memorizing facts for tests and they do not have the ability to notice their very special skills and characteristics. These are things they do so well—things that seem so easy and natural—that they go unseen, unrecognized, and eventually, become irrelevant to the student's perspective of the required skills for success in life.

The DG questions also create the ability for students to connect and transfer any of their academic skills into the world. Often, they do not understand their value.

Once we complete the DG questions, we will spend more time discussing their responses and how they feel about their life in the future now that we have identified skills or qualities of their character that will ensure success for them.

THE GIFT THAT KEEPS ON GIVING

As this session is coming to an end, I will ask the student/client to self-reflect again. As I stated in the previous chapter, every session plenary is used for self-reflection. What did they learn about themselves today? What did they celebrate about themselves? What are they acknowledging about themselves today that they may not have recognized before or perhaps have taken for granted? Always give the student some quiet self-reflecting time before you encourage them to give you their key learnings.

As they are quietly packing themselves up, I enjoy throwing in a few final questions for my young client. Prepare yourself—as I have already stated, this work is for the bold and the brave, and my final question proves this.

Just when they think that they are packing up to leave, I will ask, 'What did you notice in this session that may be holding you back and how does this habit creep into your life at school and outside of school?'

They will respond or maybe they will say, 'I never thought about that.'

If they respond, I will then ask, 'Are you ready to release it? What if you could leave it with me; how would your dream life be supported by you? What would be possible in your dream life because you left this habit with Maria today?' Most will not be able to answer this, and I ask it because I want them to be thinking of this when they leave the session and continue to think about it both consciously and unconsciously. Eventually, they will find their answer and when they do, they will share it with me.

SUMMARY OF THE GIFT STAGE:

✓ Continue building rapport with the student/client.

✓ Using your previous session notes, recap what their dream life is like.

✓ Educate, normalize, and reinforce the 'gift'.

✓ Use the DG questions to help the student begin to identify what their gifts are.

✓ Anchor the gifts by asking the student/client to reinforce how these gifts will benefit their future dream life.

✓ Use the plenary of the session to anchor their uniqueness and release any habits that do not serve them in both their life now and their dream life.

✓ Remember to take notes from today's session that will be useful in their next session with you.

CHAPTER THREE

What Are Your Values?

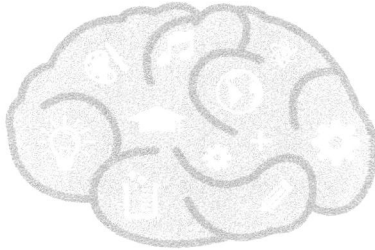

Whenever I meet a new client/student, I am consciously listening to their discussions, stories, and academic journey. Mostly, I am trying to discern subtle messages that show evidence of their core values. An individual's core values are another element of their unique imprint on the world.

As part of the requirements of my initial coaching training, learning to elicit and understand core values was an important module. We were taught the process of understanding the client's core values. This was probably the hardest module of my training and it has taken me a very long time and many hours of practice to finally elicit with confidence. With time and experience, I have now become able to identify pieces of an individual's core values just by observing their storytelling and listening to the adventures they tell me about their life.

Values are not as simple to identify as many believe they are.

Values are not words such as 'money' or 'family'. Values are words that clearly define important characteristics for us. In fact, our values can and do make or break relationships, decisions, and life journey expectations.

As this book was created to inspire you to start this work with teenagers in your school or community, I will only briefly clarify some value theory in this chapter. The purpose of this introduction is solely to ensure that we are both on the same plane of understanding where values are concerned.

Core values—in my own words—are those things that we use to judge the world and ourselves. Regardless of whom we surround ourselves with or where we work or study, these core values are primarily important to us and we will make decisions either consciously or unconsciously based on our value compass. Our internal compass is driven by our core values. It is important to remember that our values are not political, religious, or cultural beliefs; they are our ever-constant internal judgment drivers, which we use to make life decisions and guide how we live our lives.

Studies in coaching have proven that by the age of 7 years, a child's core values have been formed. Since the beginning of my training as a coach, I was never really convinced that our belief system—the one that is designed by culture, religion, society, and the major key players in our lives, such as our parents—was a separate entity from our core values. Surely, I thought our core values must be influenced by our belief system. However, without doing any proper research into this, I can only discuss this topic by using my professional and personal experience. From the Maria Vitoratos perspective, our core values are inspired by our beliefs but they are not completely defined by them. In fact, I believe—and I risk sounding very spiritual here but I cannot see any other way to describe this—our values are our soul's way of talking to us.

Most people have never identified their core values and mistake them for their beliefs. However, in a proper coaching session, I will elicit core values and without a doubt, in every session, the client is always awestruck by how empowered they feel because everything finally makes sense. Suddenly, every disagreement, disappointment, and relationship or employment breakdown makes sense. This is the evidence that I have witnessed in my clients and if I use my life as an example, my decision to leave my teaching career in late 2007 was based on my learnings from my values session with my coach. I realized why I was unfulfilled in my teaching career and the elements of my work that were no longer helping me thrive.

It is only when we clearly identify our values that we begin to live our lives totally consciously and aware of our decisions. Until this point, we are walking blindly on our path with our beliefs directing the way and as with every religious, cultural, or societal belief, they do so in a very assertive and sometimes very aggressive manner that ensures coherence and complete compliance. At times, our belief system will bully us to behave appropriately if required.

THEY SAY, WE SAY

When I first started my coaching practice in 2008, I specialized in relationships between teens and parents. Most often, the mothers would contact me and share a major concern about their teenager. The coaching was aimed at mediating and enabling better communication at home between parents and their children.

As I began to work with more and more families, I noticed some common patterns. With the risk of sounding judgmental, the mothers seemed to believe that Maria would come home and direct their teenager to follow and abide by Mum's rules and wishes. This was never the case. In fact, I was always very clear about my approach right from the initial conversation. My aim is never to tell teenagers what to do; it is to begin to understand their values and how their beliefs may be challenging their family relationships.

In my time with the families I worked with and due to the nature of my entry into the family unit, I noticed that it was not uncommon for teenagers and their parents to disagree with each other, and their disagreements were never a gentle conflict when I was invited into their lives and homes. There were many deeply seeded issues, and on the surface, to the parents, it was concerning and sometimes very heartbreaking. I am always positive about repairing parent/teen relationships because as I have witnessed, conflict resolutions are always found in the understanding of each of their core values as individuals as well as their shared family values.

What most parents do not understand—and it is very important to remember—is that the key to a great relationship with your children is the understanding and acceptance that we have unique values, and so do they. As parents, we assume that our children should and will share the same values, but this is not the case. As primary guardians, you may try to teach and instill your religious and cultural beliefs on your children, as they were instilled in you by your elders and role models, but their core values are not going to be the same. Do not misunderstand this theory; they will have similar family values on a basic level, but they will also have differing core ones.

I believe that the aim of parenting is to ensure that we are raising conscious and aware young adults who will become empowering adults who will live, work, and develop our world.

My aim in every family mediation coaching is to simply allow each member of the family to express their values and share the meaning of their values and how they align with the family unit to each other without the risk of judgment or being told that they are right or wrong.

In the next section of this chapter, I will describe my method to elicit values with teenagers and the way I use core values for teen and family empowerment.

THE VALUES STRATEGY

Every experienced coach will agree that the key to successful coaching is a buy-in from all members involved in the coaching relationship. Anyone involved who has not fully accepted or completely chosen to be coached will—in the best-case scenario—spend the coaching session awaiting an epiphany of some sort, or—in the worst-case scenario—spend their time finding evidence that the coaching is a waste of their time. I have seen this happen with teenagers and adults alike.

A coaching buy-in is the only way that the coaching magic will happen naturally. However, when a student walks into my office after making the appointment, I can see that there is an initial buy-in, even if they are not completely convinced that the coaching will be effective. It is also important to remember that by the time the student has arrived for their values session, we have already had three previous sessions; there was the initial consultation session, the 'dreaming' session, and the 'gift' session. For a student to return for this 'values' session, we are already on the road to empowerment. Let it be understood that I do not always follow the session structure as described. There are times when I know the teen may need a quick buy-in before they are ready to dream or identify their gift, so I will jump into a values session first.

THE VALUES JOURNEY

Most of what I will describe in this next section is based on the different ways I have learned to elicit values with both adults and teenagers. In fact, I have also used this approach with couples and teams.

Joanne Simpson was my Values Guru, as well as my first coaching educator. I give Joanne credit for my values knowledge and for my ability to see the importance in doing a values session with all my clients. Without her passion, I may not have recognized the great learning experience of these sessions and my clients would not have experienced these empowering sessions as well.

In my experience, my clients—regardless of age—struggle to give me a list of their values without calling out 'chunk words'. These are words such as 'family', 'money', and 'health'. These words do not describe our values but rather give us a title for things that are a return investment for some of our values.

The approach I have been using, which is very successful, is one that allows the client/teen to focus on what they do not like. I ask them to make a list of as many words or short phrases that describe the characteristics or qualities of things they do not appreciate or tolerate in other people. The purpose of this exercise is to initiate the values discovery hidden under the complaint. At first, most people may get uncomfortable; I believe that it is more about being polite and struggling to say aloud the things that they don't like in others. Remember, coaching is about self-awareness and many times, the biggest self-awareness comes from vocalizing things such as these.

My values session is one that is very structured. It is a timed event. The reason for this is that we do not want the client to be stuck on the story at this stage. I will give my client no more than three minutes for this part of the session.

Moving on from here is when the session begins to get real. I now ask my client to flip their complaint into something that they want. I ask them to imagine a coin and tell them that on one side of the coin is the complaint—the quality that they do not want to tolerate—but on the other side of the coin is the quality that they want and will always expect from others. The next five minutes are about flipping the complaints into the qualities that they want from the people they surround themselves with. It is important to remember that we are asking the teenager to elicit their core values. Therefore, when they are flipping, it is necessary to remind them that they are flipping for qualities that they would expect from people in their everyday lives and not in a specific area of their life, such as school.

As you can see, the student has a very active role in their values session. It is not one that allows them to sit and talk. Sessions with Maria are never for the passive client or student. Change happens when the individual is an active participant. As educators, we find this very easy because we are trained, and we are always expected to encourage active participation in our classrooms. Coaching is no different; for me, it is an extension of the skills I have been trained to use in my classroom.

Moving forward from the flip side, I now ask my client to allow me to take the driver's seat and ask them to enjoy being the active passenger. It is at this stage that I take their flips and start to elicit the meaning of each flipped quality or characteristic. This is the longest part of the session and can sometimes take about forty-five minutes.

When I first started my practice, I would use two sessions for the values elicitation, but time and experience has taught me how to use my time effectively—as it will for you as well. If I could offer one of my most important learnings as a coach, it is to use your gut instinct and listen carefully to the clues that your client/teen gives you to know when they have completed their thought on a quality or characteristic. There is such a thing as overkill—I should know; I have the copyright! When I was a newly qualified coach, I was always afraid of not eliciting enough and at times, I over-elicited. Okay, I'm lying; I overkilled the elicitation sessions. But with experience, I learned that the post-session homework with the client is the time for them to reflect and they will let you know if you missed anything or they want to change anything. Trust in your skills and know that if it is important, they will add it in.

Another key element of the coaching journey is to always remember that the biggest learnings happen between sessions. Our role is to help our students see the light of change; their role is to activate the light switch!

Once the meanings have all been clarified, I take the student through a fast-paced exercise wherein I read the meanings they have given me out loud. I then ask them to give each meaning a title. Most times, I ask them to imagine that we are writing their personal biography, that one of their chapters will be 'core values', and that each of their values will be a subchapter. To complete the chapter, we need a subchapter title, and each value will be just that. For some students, the title may be a word or phrase from the meanings they have created; for others, it may be something completely different. This is not important to the coach; the only person that this must make sense to is the client. Voila! The value is identified.

The next step in our session is the plenary, as always; it is when the student is asked to identify their greatest learning about themselves from the session. What are they leaving with that has either been magnified or has just been discovered? Give them a minute to reflect and then share.

I have experienced students who have told me they never realized how important these things were to them, and I have also experienced students telling me that they already knew these things. As the coach, it is not personal, and their self-reflection is not a criticism of your coaching but rather an acknowledgment of their self-reflection.

At this point, you may be asking me how the students can benefit from a values session, especially at this stage in their lives. My response is that it is HUGELY VALUABLE and in fact, this session encourages students to move away from following the traditional path of just doing what they already do and move on to consciously making career discoveries that will allow them to choose a career and post-college/high school journey.

THE VALUES-CONSCIOUS PLAN FOR THE FUTURE

It is at this stage of my coaching program that I become more homework-driven than I have been in previous sessions with the students. My focus for career development becomes very clear.

I will send my young client away with a copy of the notes that I have taken throughout the session and ask them to reflect on their values. I tell them to answer a few questions:

1. In what areas of your life do you feel you are not surrounding yourself with people who are supportive of your values?

2. What could you achieve if you surrounded yourself with empowering people who will help you strive and thrive within your values?

3. Think about your DREAM life and ask yourself: Which value is screaming out for attention to make this life possible?

4. Which value is feeding your GIFT? Which value needs more attention for your GIFT to come alive?

5. When we live our lives according to our values, we can be the best version of ourselves. What kind of post-college/high school journey would help you thrive, according to your values?

There are many more questions that I could ask—and in fact, as I am typing this, I have been inspired to ask another twenty—but as a wise teacher often reminds me, 'Less is more, Maria.' In this case, I will agree and leave it to my top five questions.

This homework is very important, and the student's responses are the conversation starter for our next session.

SUMMARY OF THE VALUES SESSION:

✓ The rapport is getting stronger, so keep building it!

✓ Normalize, normalize, normalize the challenges of being in the client's shoes, especially for teenagers.

✓ Keep track of time for every step of this session. Time is key!

✓ Recap the previous session and ask them what they have been thinking about vis-à-vis their gift and the dream.

✓ Do some brief values theory education and share the benefits of living a life by their core values.

✓ Ask the student to make a list of qualities or characteristics they cannot tolerate in other people.

✓ Flip the negatives into qualities or characteristics they

want to see in the people they surround themselves with in their everyday lives.

✓ Elicit the meaning of the qualities and stop when your gut instinct tells you that the teen has completely expressed themselves.

✓ Do a quick-fire reading of their meanings and ask the student to give you a title for every meaning. The title becomes the value!

✓ End your session with some self-reflection and send them away with a list of questions that will allow them to anchor their values awareness and the career path they will begin to take with your coaching.

Chapter Four

Your Value is Not Defined by Your Grades

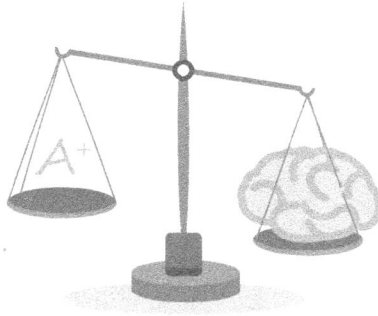

Young adults today have challenges that youth of my generation didn't have. The competition is fierce, and our teens have gotten the idea that their grades will define their worldly value. Working in a high school and parenting a teenage daughter, I see just how defining grades are for our youth. When did this happen and why are we, as a society, allowing it to overpower our teenagers?

Essentially, as I see it, we are allowing grades to define the empowerment of our future leaders. I have seen young adults walking around like academic zombies. They study and do tests but the drive and passion for learning and curiosity is *very limited and in some cases non-existent.*

With every teen that I have met—my daughter included—I have seen and heard their concerns and overwhelming fear of the stress that seems to overpower their young lives. I see them wonder, 'Will I get into university? Am I a stronger candidate then my peers? Will I be able to make my parents proud of me?'

However, to many educators and parents across the globe, the stress and academic pressure that exists for teens is not as serious as they make it out to be. One of the most common comments that I have heard in adult discussions that involve the topic of teenagers in schools is that 'no one said that life was going to be easy; they just have to stop playing around and focus on their studies.' Although this sounds like an easy judgment to make, if we are expecting the world to be a peaceful place, I believe that as mentors, role models, and teen empowerment leaders, we must have more empathy for our young adults. I believe—and my work with teens confirms this—that it is vital to understand and empathize with the feelings of our adolescents. We must validate their stress levels and help them find validation in the work they are doing in high school. I do agree that the world is not a bubble of kindness and love filled with equal opportunities for everyone; however, I do not agree that just because the world is a place filled with challenges and unequal opportunities, we must continue down this path when educating our young adults.

This next chapter is one that was created to inspire you—the educator, the parent, or the leader of teen empowerment—to have a different perspective than the one that societies across the Western world seem to have blindly adopted. It is my highest hope that you will end this chapter wanting to continue sharing the message that 'your value is not defined by your grades.'

Part of this chapter's mission is to ask you questions that trigger your curiosity. Is 'value = grades' a message that we really want to be sending teenagers today? For some—parents included—grades are the measure of success for the investment that we are making in our students, while for others, grades are just a symbol of good study habits but carry very little meaning in relation to the real world. However, with tertiary education not budging in their measures of entry to their institutes, what are we really defining with grades?

Depression, suicide, and self-harm are some of the side effects of teen stress that have been correlated to academic pressures in high school students in the US, Canada, the UK, and Australia. According to the World Health Organization, depression has become a common illness suffered by 300 million people worldwide and counting. The WHO statistics (as of February 2017) state that young teenagers (13 and up) who have begun to show signs of depression are on the rise.

Why am I stating this fact? For purely selfish reasons, of course: I want to create a great debate. I want to create a wave of action that continues the debate until our teenagers believe their grades do not, and will never, define their value.

So, how are we handling this on an educational level? Aside from the statistics and the holistic views of a work/life balance, how are we equipping our young adults to handle stress-triggering behavior? In my opinion, we are not. In fact, the tertiary education system is contributing to it unnecessarily. Why is an 'A' the defining grade for a teenager's entry into university education? What exactly are we testing them for? Does any of the high school knowledge contribute to the first-year university student's success? If this is true, then why do an overwhelming number of university students fail within their first semester at university? Does the A-grade offer any guarantee to the parents of these children that they will succeed at life after college? Definitely not.

With a bold statement such as the one that I am making, I do recognize that there are wonderful initiatives taking place in schools across the globe. In fact, well-being and mindfulness has caught on quite well in many schools and it seems to be the new fashion or high schools to implement programs that teach mindfulness with the aim of strengthening students' well-being. Sadly, however, the tertiary education systems still require that our students sit assessments that are meant to decide the academic fate of our young people and their post-high school education.

For some students, grades will even define the type of career they may choose. Who are we to decide that a 17-year-old who is not achieving the A-grade cannot be a genius aero-nautical engineer in her future? These academic grades are a heavily defining moment with many hours of lost sleep, im-proper nutrition, and declining mental states for our teenag-ers, their parents, and their teachers.

An even larger issue on our hands is: Are the grades of our students defining not only their value, but the value of our edu-cators as well? What is the reality of the messages we are send-ing to the world? How consciously aware of these messages are we? On the one hand, we have a rising epidemic of depression, and on the other, we are feeding into the levels of unnecessary stress on our young adults. When and where does this all stop?

RANT OVER; NOW WHAT?

When my young clients re-enter my office for their post-values coaching session, we discuss their core values. In doing so, we spend some time reflecting on how their academic behavior and the peers they surround themselves with align with those values. Usually, there is a big pause before they respond. I encourage the pause, because within this pause comes the real self-awareness and self-reflection of the individual.

This exercise is as powerful as looking into the mirror and noticing our imperfections. As I have stated and will continue to state numerous times throughout this book, coaching is not for the weak-hearted. Coaching is about noticing our habits and recognizing which ones are serving our highest benefits and which ones are no longer serving us.

Once the student has begun to recognize their habits and the alignment of their life behaviors with their values, we are able to have a discussion that involves their hopes and fears in relation to their academic journey. This session is more about normalizing and reinstalling the idea of belief and potential for the future with the student.

It has been clear to me throughout my experience working as a coach with young people that teenagers today are afraid of failure—and I am not referring to failing a course or assignment. Our teenagers are correlating their grades with their life's worth and in effect, they are also defining their human worth in relation to their grades. If I were given a pine tree seedling for every teenager that I consoled in these sessions who felt this way, I would be able to plant a forest of trees today.

As I have seen in my experience working with teenagers, the future leaders of tomorrow are struggling with self-confidence and I am convinced that this low confidence is feeding into their mindset and is rolling into their academic achievement as well.

Over six years ago today, I did a very small-scale research project called 'Back to School'. I interviewed thirty young people from the ages of four to nineteen. I wanted to discover if there was an actual connection between academic achievement and peer/teacher relationships. The results were overwhelmingly similar in the respect that our young people cannot focus on their academic studies if they are not in the right mindset. As educators and parents, we have a strong responsibility and obligation to help them feel empowered and limitless in their capabilities.

I recognize that there are students who do not take responsibility for their learning and many who do not even appreciate the wonderful learning opportunities that are offered to them. As a coach, educator, and mother of three very different children, I understand the frustrations that we have with young adults; however, isn't this part of their life journey? Aren't they learning how to develop their attitudes and behaviors? Isn't the purpose of school life and everyday life to enrich their reactions to the life lessons that are put in front of them?

TELL THEM, SHOW THEM, REPEAT

A teenager may roll their eyes or even tear up because they do not believe they are better than their grade on a chemistry test. Never stop telling them just how wonderful they are.

Never stop showing them the opportunities that a C-grade can offer them. Use every opportunity to enlighten the young adult in your office or in your classroom. They need it but most importantly, they deserve it. They really need the encouragement.

Unlike teenagers from the past, teens today are struggling with the boxes and labels we have created because we believed that striving for the best would create the best. My question and the great debate is: What is the risk we are taking with the future of our young people? Do these competitive labels have more power over their mindset than necessary? What are the rewards for the teen, their family, and society? An A-grade? The entry to an Ivy League university? Teenage depression? Self-harm? Masks of happiness hiding the anxieties of children?

Believe me when I say this; our teenagers have enough examples to remind them they are living in a world of great competition full of challenges and struggles. They do not need more teachers, coaches, or parents repeating this fact.

I view this discussion in my office with a teenager as one that allows me the opportunity to invest time, energy, and love into a human being who will one day rise above every difficulty that came with being a student and feel like somebody important at the most impressionable time in their lives. Whether they become a neurosurgeon who finds a cure for Alzheimer's or a teller at the local supermarket, this young person will wake up feeling like life helped them thrive in the decisions that they made for their future.

Our teenagers must be educated to thrive because if they continue to label themselves as a success or a failure based on their grades, then what does this say about us as role models? Would you rate the value of your spouse or your parent based on their income? What about their job title? If this were the case, then I would like to raise the great debate and start a mission to redefine our human values because I cannot live on a planet that allows our young people—the very people who will find cures for disease and change the face of politics—to feel like they are defined by a letter on a piece of paper. If there is ever a chance for world peace, there is a teenager sitting in your office or your classroom right now with the power to achieve this great feat!

Tell your teens that they have the power to make substantial changes in their life. Show them how to turn the habits of ineffective studying into the habits of successful and effective studying. Tell them how you achieved success and show them the steps that you have taken to get from where they are today to where you are today. Our teenagers deserve discussions that allow them to realize that their value is not measured by their grades. Failure on a test does not equate to failure in life.

Start this mission and make it the norm at your school. Make it the expectation in your community. Encourage this discussion with other high schools in your area. Bring the working world on board with this mission, for it is the mission of us all. The future of our world depends heavily on the mindset of our young people.

Telling teens that their value should never be defined by their grades is a more challenging element of the work we do with them. When we infuse belief and self confidence in others, we are first trying to balance the past beliefs of the individual. This is very difficult. Studies that discuss the brain and its ability to suppress information in the subconscious have shown us that what we believe about ourselves and the impact left behind from past experiences is not always hovering on the surface. There is an iceberg of feelings that dig far deeper below the surface than we can imagine.

Of course, teenagers are young, and they shouldn't have so many deep-rooted issues, but the truth is that many do. For most, they have been in school since the early age of about four years old with teachers, parents, and role models teaching them by telling them all the things they are doing wrong. After all, isn't it important to teach them by telling them their mistakes? Many adults and educators believe this to be the most effective teaching method. I, on the other hand, disagree. I believe that the 'Tell Them, Show Them' method involves telling them when they are doing something well and showing them how they can make it even better. An empowered future requires an empowered method of teaching and learning.

Do not misunderstand; I am not advocating a false sense of greatness in our teens. On the contrary, I am promoting an empowered method of teaching them how to improve their skills and abilities without breaking them down or further destroying their already delicate mindset.

Summary of Your Value
is Not Defined by Your Grades

✓ Normalize the issue of grades vs personal value. Normalizing will help the teen to understand that they are not alone in their fear.

✓ Bring their fears to the surface. Call them out, investigate them, and give the teen the time to share them with you.

✓ Discuss their core values and give the student time to reflect on their habits and academic behavior. Are the decisions they make and the people they surround themselves with aligned with their core values?

✓ Tell them, show them, and repeat. Teens today have been fed negativity since the start of their academic journey (since they were about four years old). Tell them again and again just how much potential they have. Show them how to improve and tell them stories about successful people who could've failed because of their academic underachievement. Repeat and repeat until they believe it.

✓ Show your teen how to go from their present stance to their grand potential.

✓ This does not end with the end of the session. I believe that this session is a conversation that continues and never ends. I believe that we pass the torch from adult to adult until our young teenager can pick themselves up and keep moving forward, regardless of their grades.

CHAPTER FIVE

Do You Have What It Takes to Bring Out Your Greatness?

D enial is the greatest obstacle for clients from the ages of six to sixty-five—myself included. What is denial? How does it fit into this chapter, let alone into this book at all? I believe that denial is at the core of most of our challenges as human beings. I believe that denial is the grey boundary that allows one to cross over from unskilled to skilled and empowered.

The next two chapters are all about my personal and professional learnings which offer my students, my young clients, and my own children special skills and tools to help feed their minds, develop their skills, and find ways to discover their potential. I believe this will help lift them up and give them the strength to fly into their future selves.

I invite you to enjoy the following pages and I hope they will inspire your own self-reflection and conversations with your teenagers that will help them thrive. It is in the thriving that the driving begins and we all know that when we are driving, there is always the exciting potential for an amazing ride.

WHAT IS GREATNESS AND HOW DO WE ACHIEVE IT?

The dictionary definition of 'greatness' is the quality of being great and having distinction.

As I sit writing these words, I ask myself the same question again and again. Is greatness a realistic expectation? Are we aspiring to the achievement of something that is truly un-reachable? As adults in the corporate world and beyond, I have seen many still striving to achieve the bare minimum. How do we expect our young teenagers to aim for greatness?

With the last chapter still lingering on my mind, the constant teen expectation is that the A-grade will be a sign of great-ness in their world, thus instilling the assumption that their A-grade is a defining factor of their human value. Are we en-couraging more opportunities for them to fall off the edge of greatness? Are we advocating more grade-defining boundar-ies that set them up to fail?

I disagree. I believe that greatness is not about the grade. Greatness is not a box to fit into and with this, I claim that greatness is not the same for everyone. In fact, greatness is different and special for every individual, regardless of their age. We define our own greatness. With this belief, we are in the driver's seat and we are reliant upon our successful achievement of greatness.

Allow me to explain this theory in more depth.

When a student returns for their 'Greatness Session', I will always begin by asking them how they have been feeling since our last session together. It is important to remember that the last four sessions have been very deep learning experiences for the student. I spend time with them discussing their self-reflections. I encourage a dialogue of: What thoughts have crept into your mind since our last session together? What worries and fears have been created in your mind or become even larger for you? Beginning your session this way always reminds the young client that our journey is one of continuation and past learnings are most empowering when we reflect on them.

Moving on from the self-reflection process of this session, I spend time doing some motivation and normalizing again. If you remember anything from this book, I hope that it is the practice of normalizing for the teenager in every session. This should not be done lightly. Teenagers are struggling deeply with the fear of 'standing out unnecessarily amongst their peers' and so, normalizing situations and circumstances helps calm their fears and helps them feel 'normal'. Quite frankly, 'normal' for them means that there is nothing wrong with them.

The 'Greatness Session' is a conversation that encourages the student to feed their mind with empowerment in high doses. They are ready for it. The last session gave them the required appetizers and now they can eat the main course: Greatness.

This is a make-or-break session; it will either help them fly forward and reach for the stars or it won't. In my practice, this conversation is like a dance wherein the music has a varied tempo from slow to fast and anywhere in between. As coaches, we are trained to 'dance in the moment', and this session is a perfect example of doing just that.

The dance starts with taking some steps backward to the consultation session. This was when the student came to coaching either because they were encouraged by a parent or teacher or they were curious and came in of their own accord. We discuss how they initially felt coming to my sessions. We only spend a few minutes here and never get stuck in this place.

Shifting up the tempo slightly, we then leap into their DREAM LIFE and discuss just how lovely they will be in that world. In fact, I call it just that—'your future world'. Doing this helps the student believe that although at the moment, it is still a dream, they are also brave enough to create the dream because in that world, fear does not exist. As I begin to see the student climbing higher up the ladder of confidence and belief, we discuss their core values. Once again, we never get stuck in this tempo.

Doing a quick value recap helps us define what sets this teenager apart from the rest of the world. It is very important during the 'Greatness Session' that the individual is able to identify their uniqueness with confidence. Doing so allows them to believe even more in their own greatness.

As we keep the dance moving, we are sharing dreams and values and always celebrating the journey they have taken. I believe that great people are grateful people who celebrate every step they have taken. Regardless of their grades or their success as defined by teachers or guardians, every step forward is just that—a STEP FORWARD. We celebrate.

Self-reflection comes in twice during this session; the dance slows down to a gentle pause wherein I ask the student to pause and notice the progress they are making in their life. I then ask them to pause again and look ahead into their future. What does the DREAM life ask of them? What gift do they have that may or may not be completely developed? Never rush the student during these pauses; this part of the dance requires a slow tempo, and the need to rush is nature's way of calling out fear and anxiety.

ONE SIZE DOES NOT FIT ALL

When I work with clients, students, or even just discuss my work with my fellow colleagues, I never hide my passion for greatness. Although I may not be everyone's cup of tea, I would rather deliver the enthusiasm for this work then accept playing small while trying to please everyone.

As the title of this subchapter suggests, one size does not fit all but I have never stated, nor do I believe, that greatness is one size fits all, either. However, I do believe that just as a pine tree starts as a seedling, so does greatness. Words of encouragement are just this—seedlings for greatness. They come from my core. They are born from a place within me that only seems to exist naturally when I walk the path that this work has taken me on. This is my purpose and I feel great doing it. I feel great watching it unfold. I hope this chapter brings out this feeling in you as well. Our teens need it. They truly deserve it.

In my experience as a coach, a Mum, and a teacher, teenagers are uncomfortable and do not want to stand out—unless, of course, it is within the norm that is seen as acceptable by their trend-driving peers. Therefore, the theory of greatness seems to conflict with many teens. Greatness requires that they stand out and show distinction. This is an incredibly challenging task for most adults, let alone most teenagers. Standing up and claiming distinction leaves us vulnerable to criticism and showing vulnerability means that we allow ourselves to be open to critics.

In my practice, mentoring and coaching go hand-in-hand during this session with a teen. I tend to bounce from coach to mentor and back again. However, as I change hats, I will always ask for permission. An experienced coach must always remember that we are there to encourage the client to think outside the box and we are not in the room to tell them what works best for their lives. We are not the expert in their lives, they are. In fact, in my opinion, not all coaches can justify being a mentor in the greatness session, either. I, however, feel very equipped to. Yes, I am boldly declaring my greatness. Let me explain.

I am a former educator who took a huge leap of faith in 2008 and resigned her post as a comfortable teacher who was earning a very generous income. I did this to open a coaching company with no prior business experience and only a fresh coaching diploma with my name printed on it as evidence that I could be so bold. I walked the path of discomfort and did so with considerable pride—and on most days, with considerable fear, as well. I cried most days because I feared failure. Every day offered me new challenges. My identity as a successful professional was being battered and abused. I was clearly no different than most who had made a career change. Most mornings, I would wake up feeling emotionally connected to my work but most days, the challenges of running a successful business saw me close my eyes at night feeling great worry for its survival. The edge I seemed to have crossed was steeper than I expected it to be when I resigned.

As with every change, my growth spurt, as well as my path of change and intense discomfort, saw me grow both professionally and personally. All aspects of my life were being affected by my career change and I had to accept the changes and stay on the path—or I could always choose to turn back and reapply for a teaching post. As with most great people, the path of greatness was not smooth. There were more unseen pitfalls than were ever described to me. The journey of greatness was constantly one of intense uncertainty. Every day, I—just as every individual on the same path—had to be prepared to stand in the fire of fear and follow through with only my core values as the torch that could lead the way. There were always times when my ego would feed me toxic thoughts which almost made me so weak that even the words of an empowering mentor could not override them.

I remember one specific moment on my journey when I sat down with my mentor—who I can now look back upon with gratitude—and she told me that I was an active participant in my decision to change careers and I was not a victim. She gave me tough love and taught me to stand up again and face the challenge or turn back and return to my comfort zone. The magic that happened for me after this mentoring session was larger than life. There was a bittersweet feeling wherein

I thanked her out loud and hated her silently. I didn't understand her tough love then, but looking back, if she allowed me to cry and feel self-pity in that moment, I would never be standing where I am right now.

My work since that conversation has impacted at least 3000 teenagers that I am aware of, but I am certain that the domino effect of conversations I have had with teachers, parents, and teenagers, articles I have written, television and radio interviews I have participated in, and events I have created has impacted many more teens across my region and potentially even the world.

My mentor was able to capture my essence of greatness because she walked my path. I trusted her because I knew she was talking from a place of authenticity and not a throne of wisdom high above the rubble of challenge. I will repeat again: As we have already discussed, greatness is not for the weak-hearted; it is for the individuals who are standing in the fire and staying there because they know that in the process of melting, change is happening, and greatness is the result of change. Unless the coach has undergone such a path of greatness, they cannot be a mentor of greatness.

In this case, I will encourage you to find a teenager to mentor for greatness, because they need to feel the energy that only a greatness graduate can offer them. The energy of great people comes from their core and not from their surface. There is a light in their eyes that identifies them. Have you seen it? Can you see it in yourself? I have seen it in many people; I have seen it in teens, and my aim is to see it in everyone who walks my path on this journey.

QUESTIONS TO ASK DURING THE GREATNESS SESSION:

1. When you say yes to greatness, what do you say no to?

2. When you feel afraid of showing your distinction, what does the greatness within you ask for?

3. When you feel like giving up on being different, what would your dream life ask you to do?

4. When you want to be great, but you feel the audience is uncomfortable with it, what is your gift asking you to remember?

5. When you feel weak and you want to give up or back down, what would your cheerleader ask you to do?

6. When greatness is calling you, will you take the call? What might stop you? How will you take the lead and rise to your greatness?

BRINGING THE GREATNESS TOGETHER

As this session ends, the student is requested to identify their glimmer of greatness. For some students, this session may involve watching a greatness role model in action and then asking them to identify the strategies used that have made the person great. For other students, it will be a session of asking them to identify habits and behaviors that they have witnessed from their 'greatness role model'. For many, this session will require a lot of mentoring from the core of greatness. Speaking to the young adult from a place where the ego has no space, and talking to them with authenticity is essential. Greatness needs no audience to identify it as great;

it only needs the light to shine bright and warm on anyone in its presence.

The students will leave this session feeling energized and empowered with a strong belief that they can do it. They will leave with an inner knowledge that their dreams, gifts, core values, and uniqueness are the recipe that has created their greatness. They will leave feeling capable of anything and everything. They will be able to look past their grades and look ahead into their bright future—the place that greatness will lead them to. As a coach witnessing a session such as this one, it is indescribable. The feeling is overwhelming. I hope you will all be able to experience such a session with your teen clients. It truly feels like floating on a magical wave of effortless energy that takes you to a place where anything is possible.

SUMMARY OF DO YOU HAVE WHAT IT TAKES TO BRING OUT YOUR GREATNESS?

✓ Discuss and clarify what 'denial' is and how it is a core challenge to the achievement of one's full potential.

✓ Discuss what 'greatness' entails and how it can be achieved.

✓ Remember and remind your coachee that 'one size does not fit all' for greatness. Celebrate their uniqueness!

✓ Brighten the glimmer of greatness by identifying the qualities of a 'Greatness Role Model' and inspire your young client to believe that they, too, are capable of greatness.

CHAPTER SIX

YOUR SERMON WILL BE
YOUR GUIDE IF YOU LET IT

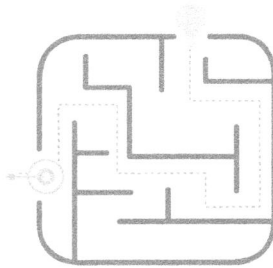

Young or old, this chapter is all about looking backwards and connecting the dots. It is about helping our teenagers step outside their present story and take a journey into the far, far future. With the world as it is in its present state, assuming that we have years and years to live should no longer be a factor in our lives. I believe that our children—as well as ourselves—should begin with the end in mind.

It is in this chapter that I will demonstrate how I use this session to help my young clients begin to identify their purpose. The pages that lay ahead of us will potentially trigger you to feel one of two emotions: Fear or inspiration. I believe that both emotions will lead you to the destination that is at the root of your potential. However, I must warn you: Depending on your habits, procrastination is always a possibility. The work is not in discovering the destination, but rather the journey that is required to make the impossible possible.

As you read through the chapter ahead, please remember that age is not a factor and the work in this chapter can and has been successful with children as young as ten years old in my practice. I believe that the younger the child, the stronger their belief in the possibility of grand purposes. Do not limit your students based on the limitations that you have grown to believe exist.

Is the Casket Open or Closed?

Imagine that you are in a room filled with every person that has ever crossed your life path. They have all gathered to pay their respects to your life. Every one of them has a short tale about the impact that you made on them. Every one of them will share these stories aloud. You are the guest of honor, but at this gathering, you do not have a physical form. In fact, you are dead, and no one knows that you are even in the room.

As you listen to their stories about your impact during your lifetime, focus on the words they are using to describe you. What are they saying? How have you inspired them—or was it quite the opposite? Watch the faces in the room. Listen to the reactions of the guests as they listen to the stories about you. Are you happy listening to them? Are they describing you just as you hoped they would?

Just as the gathering is beginning to end, a small child walks into the room and begins sharing their story. The child is roughly five years old. Listen carefully. The child is telling everyone about your hopes and dreams. The child is telling everyone about the possibilities they saw in you. The child is sharing their emotional insights into how you felt as a human being.

You Are That Child

As you watch your younger self speaking and sharing their deepest thoughts about how you wished your life would turn out, I want you to reflect on your life right now. Are you happy? Are you hopeful? Do you feel inspired by the opportunities that lay ahead of you? Did you achieve any of your 5-year-old self's dreams and hopes yet? What did you hope that your life would become when you were a young child and how have you strayed from those ambitions?

Remember to catch your ego creating mind obstacles while you are doing this exercise. A mind obstacle is when your mind feeds you doubt and fear. It will remind you about monetary obligations, parental expectations, societal beliefs, and anything else that may stop you from dreaming. Do not allow yourself to make excuses for why or how you haven't been able to achieve any of your ambitions. Do not allow your mind to convince you that these dreams or ambitions are not possible. The purpose of this short exercise is to allow yourself to view your life as you believed it could be when the world had no impact on your dreams or the possibility of achieving your goals and ambitions.

STEP 1:

Use Column 1 to write down all your younger self's dreams, hopes, and aspirations, regardless of how unrealistic they may seem to you right now. What did you want to do before your exam results became your identity? Who did you want to become before the educational system made you believe that you had to follow the most common path? Do you remember your dress-up days? What did you pretend you would become during those playtimes? Do you remember your bedtime stories? Which stories did you want to read over and over again? Who did you wish you could become after reading those stories? Write them all down. Don't think about why they are necessary. JUST WRITE.

STEP 2:

In Column 2, we will reflect on some of the DG questions provided in the chapter on 'Greatness'. Spend as much time as you need on each question. The biggest self-awareness comes from moments of reflection. Imagine if your dreams or ambitions came true. What would your life look like today? What would it feel like to be you? Repeat these questions for everything that you have written in Column 1. Stop yourself from trying to do anything other than just answering these two questions.

STEP 3:

Column 3 is a straightforward part of this tool. Quite simply, read the dream/ambition again and then read what you wrote in Column 2. Does this ambition make you smile? Does it make you feel excited? Do you smile on the inside, imagining the life that you could have if this ambition came true? Use this column to write 'yes' or 'no'. Then write a brief sentence supporting your answer. Do not dwell too long on this column. Your ego will feed on the negative, so be alert and really ask yourself 'why or why not' before you shun the dream/ambition.

STEP 4:

Only complete the ambitions that you wrote 'yes' for in Column 3 for this step. Use Column 4 to answer the next questions from the DG list. What skills do you need to adopt for this dream to come true? Do you already have these skills? If not, what can you do to learn them? What kind of personal or professional traits do you need for this dream to become viable? Do you already possess them? If not, where can you learn them?

STEP 5:

Column 5 is about your ego and the limiting beliefs that you have been holding onto. Write down all the limiting thoughts that are keeping this dream/ambition from becoming a reality. Make a list of the people or teachers who have limited you. Write down the statements that come to your mind as they are. Do not edit them. Use the words that you would tell yourself or the words that you have heard from others.

STEP 6:

Reflect over everything that you have written in the columns. Read the columns through the eyes of your '5-year-old self'. Remember: This child had no limiting beliefs. As with every child, they would have just believed in the possibility of all dreams. When you find yourself reading Column 5, become that 5-year-old again. How would they react to the statements in this column? What would this child say to the negativity? Listen to your ego as you complete Step 6. Catch yourself being limited and stop. Do not allow your mind to feed you limiting beliefs.

STEP 7:

Make a list of your fan club members. Who are the people in your life that would read your dreams and ambitions and scream out 'Go for it!'? Make a list of the teachers, family members, friends, or strangers that have been feeding you positivity. Ask yourself: What do they believe about you and your potential that you don't?

Once you have completed the seven steps, take a break and get some air. It is important to step away from self-reflection after you have completed the exercise. Your mind needs time to digest the information. I always tell my clients that the biggest learnings come between sessions. I would usually end my session at the end of Step 7 and simply ask this next question: 'What did this exercise teach you about yourself today?' However, if you wish to carry on, then you can return to it after you have taken a break.

Because this book is aimed at working with teens, the next part of this exercise will be geared towards them and their focus; however, as I have already stated, all the exercises in the book can be done with teens and adults.

STEP 8:

Reread your chart filled with the seven columns and then ask yourself this next question: 'If you knew that you could reach the dream(s) that you have written down in Column One, what or whom would you need for support?' Remind the young client that 'impossible' is NOT an answer. It is important to remember that the ego will try to put doubt and ideas of impossibility into their mind; so, as their coach, notice when doubt rises and stroke their ego by reminding it that this is only an exercise and there are no requirements for commitment.

For some teens, their response may be, 'There's no way this can come true because money/education/family support is an obstacle.' These are factors, but they are not insurmountable. Remember: The aim of Step 8 is to simply brainstorm the type of support that would make the dream easier to achieve. Answer the question and swiftly move on to Step 9.

STEP 9:

Put a timeframe on the dream. How many years would your client/student need to achieve the dream? It is important that the timeframe should be as realistic as possible. As you will notice, we are now pinning the teen into committing to a dream and turning the dream into an achievable goal. Step 9 should not take any more than a few minutes to complete. Taking too long on this step will give the ego time to creep up again.

STEP 10:

This step is the beginning of a goal strategy for achieving the dream. It is what corporate coaches would call 'Key Performance Indicators'—except in my practice working with teens, I call it 'Key Goal Achievements'. The next few sessions are your typical coaching sessions wherein you will use action coaching strategies to make this dream a reality. Dreams are not meant for the imagination with my clients. They are goals waiting to evolve.

SUMMARY OF YOUR SERMON
WILL BE YOUR GUIDE IF YOU LET IT

✓ Use the visualization technique provided. Ensure that your client is comfortable and relaxed before you begin.

✓ Recap the DG questions from the 'What is Your Gift' chapter.

✓ Complete Steps 1 through 7 and stop.

✓ Complete Steps 8 through 10 to create Key Goal Achievements.

✓ Begin action coaching and help empower their future.

CHAPTER SEVEN

If Not Now, When?

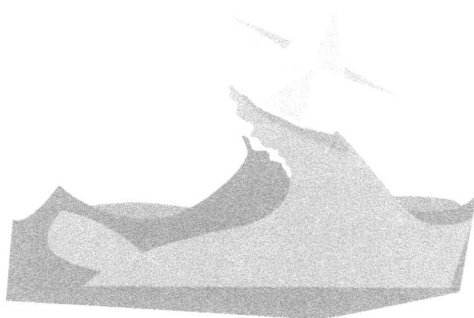

Imagine being 17 years old all over again. What would you do differently the second time around? I often think about this and my list continues to grow with each self-reflection. Whichever way I think about it, my biggest change would have to be the career or lack of career support that I received as a high school student. I remember having a guidance counsellor, but he didn't discuss careers with the students. He was seen in the school, but I do not remember him being proactive with us about anything. It is also important to note that there were about 500 students to cater to on his own. This is no easy task, regardless of how great you are at your role. It was also a generation when careers were not discussed as options with teenagers in school. I do not ever remember having a conversation with any member of the teaching staff during my high school years about careers.

I was educated in the French province of Canada called Quebec. In our province, we left high school in grade 11 (at 16 years old). Some students went on to further their studies in an academic institution called a Cegep (A-levels or IB equivalence), while others joined the workforce or first went on to learn a trade and then joined the workforce. Applying to Cegep was like the university application process, but the only conversation I can remember having with my guidance counsellor was the one in which he told me that my grades were not high enough to attend a private Cegep. His comments didn't sway me in the least and I never thought about the impact that this may have on my future.

As many students did, I went on to study in the public system and continued my academic journey into university at the end of my 2-year Cegep program. Upon completion of Cegep, I was still not given any career support. In fact, I do not even remember being introduced to any career advisor at all.

When I finally completed university, I realized that I had a wonderful piece of paper that proved how educated I was, but I had no idea what benefit this piece of paper could offer me. Unlike my very focused brother who went down the medical path, I was on the 'Bachelor of Arts' path—and by arts, I am not referring to paintbrushes and a canvas. My degree meant that I'd read a lot of books, but I didn't have any idea what I could do for employment other than work in a nursery, and this was simply because I had done a double major in Child Studies and Sociology.

To my luck, I moved to another country and fell into the primary education industry. This led me to continue my studies and for the sake of employment, I pursued a Post-Graduate Certificate in Education, which then meant that I was a qualified teacher and I was able to work in a school and teach. Was this my purpose in life? Upon reflection, I do not believe it was. Connecting my life dots, the start of my career was the key to this book coming to life.

Am I promoting a lack of career education because I turned out to be what society would deem successful? No, I am not. I imagine that—although every career step I have taken has proven very rewarding to me—I have taken a very long route and I am finally on the path to where I really want to be professionally.

What would I have done differently if I'd had more career support as a young teenager? I believe that I could have made a more informed decision about my future. Perhaps I would have followed the educational path or perhaps I would have decided to pursue interests in law, social work, management, or even journalism. I love my work and I cannot imagine what life would be like if I didn't work with teenagers or if I wasn't helping people strive to be their best. I do, however, feel that more information and support should be given to students as early as primary school.

This is a big statement, but I have 10 years and many hours of coaching teens and developing a career education curriculum to support my opinion. I have also had the opportunity to speak to professionals, parents, and teachers who have all shared their own stories of how they never had career support when they were teenagers. I have yet to meet an adult that has not voiced the wish and declaration that their life would be different if they'd had some career support and guidance when they were young.

This closing chapter is not about giving you, the reader, a tool or resource to use with your students or your teenagers. It is a chapter that is aimed at inspiring you to change your dialogue with the young adults in your life. It is meant to get you thinking about how your impact can and will make a significant difference in their future and in return, in the future of our world. I hope that by the end of these next few pages, you will close this book feeling excited and inspired to extend a hand to the future leaders under your care.

CHOICE OR OBLIGATION?

A typical conversation that I have with students when they walk into my office usually starts something like this: 'I am choosing Biology, Chemistry, Maths, and Business as my A-Levels, Maria. I don't know what I want to do for my career but studying these subjects will give me options for university. I really wanted to take art, but my parents feel that it will not be a good choice for my future. I really didn't enjoy studying Science in Year 10, but my parents told me that I have to choose realistic subjects in Sixth Form. I don't know if I want to go to university, so I'll just go and figure my career out when I graduate from university. I'll just do any course at university and figure it out later.'

With every student that walks into my office feeling depleted and powerless, I refuel and become more passionate about this work. In my mind, it is a simple equation. The self-development industry continues to rise, and motivational speakers are becoming key elements of corporate gatherings, so why are we not investing in the career education and motivation of our future employers and employees? I want to clarify what I see on a daily basis with teenagers, but I will paint this picture through the lens of the corporate world.

Picture this: It's the end of Quarter 3 and you are meeting with your line manager. They are holding your performance review and it will decide either your performance success or your professional demise. Part of this review is also to decide the budget plans for your department and your role. Your line manager does not seem impressed with your performance and asks you what has happened. You respond with, 'Well, I didn't really like my job tasks, but I thought I would wing it and everything would fall into place by the time we had this performance review.' As expected, she gives you a poor performance review and tells you that due to the nature of your work and the lack of profitability, the organization has decided they will have to downsize. You have been given your final notice. You have been fired.

This scenario is exactly what our children are doing now. In one scenario, they are not enjoying their academic choices and they are underperforming. In another, they are performing but their mental state is suffering because they are being forced to do something they don't want to do. Our teens are making choices based on the constant fear-mongering reminders of poverty and failing. However, in my experience working with teens, their greatest worry is their fear of disappointing their parents and to them, this is a much worse fate than unemployment.

'It takes a village to raise a child.'

—*African Proverb*

I have been in a room filled with parents who claim to want their children to be happy. I have also been in a room with the children of those parents, who are afraid of failing in the eyes of their parents and making academic and career choices based on their assumptions of their parent's expectations for their professional success. In fact, most teens assume that their career success will be their measure of success as a human being through the eyes of their parents and society.

Being a mother myself, I know that I want my children to be happy and successful. I do not believe that there is a parent out there who would not wish the same for their children. However, I do not want to believe that as parents, we should accept that our children feel so powerless. I will continue to believe that parents want their children to be happy, and they understand that for their children to find their happiness, they must discover the career journey that will bring their internal light to life and spark their interests, regardless of our own fears or inhibitions about their future.

Of all the strategies I have used during my work in career coaching, the most profound experiences for the students always comes when professionals visit the high school—especially when these same professionals are honest about their career journey and choices, and the real-life tasks that are required in their jobs.

For many schools, inviting guest speakers is not a new idea; in fact, it has been customary practice for many years. However, my approach to this is not traditional, to say the least. I expect and give permission to professionals to share the 'raw truth'. There is no holding back on any of these discussions. I expect that they will be honest about how they made their career choices. I expect that they will discuss salary scales, employability, and predicted trends moving forward.

However, I do not accept that the teens in the audience should sit back passively. I expect that they will be proactive and enforce this approach. I have witnessed a 13-year-old question an ophthalmologist about the impact of robotics and future employability in the next ten years. Let me tell you; our guest speaker did NOT see that question coming.

In case you are wondering, our students did not just walk into the auditorium and ask these questions at random. This program has been running for three years with a minimum of one professional speaker a week and on our dedicated 'Careers Day' with anywhere between 120-150 professionals, our students have had amble practice at listening and asking the right questions. All guests are selected by me personally. I take the time to meet them and learn about their professional growth first. I prepare them both verbally and with a speaker's guideline for their talks. I raise the bar for our students, and our speakers are always impressed.

With over 900 known careers in 2017 and hundreds more either being created or eliminated by the time our students enter the workforce, I want to ensure that they have had as much exposure to as many professionals as possible during their impressionable years at our high school. Do I only invite A-class careers? No. I want the A-Z of career professionals. It is not my right to decide which professions our students should be exposed to. Our world needs blue-collar workers as much as they white-collar workers.

COACHING VERSUS DICTATING

This book was aimed at offering you the tools and strategies I use with my young clients and students. With everything in this book, I have demonstrated that the most effective dialogue is one that uses a coaching approach.

Educators are natural coaches. In fact, during my teaching practice, we were taught to ask our students open-ended questions. The practice of coaching does just that. However, using the model created and practiced by the Co-Active Coaching Approach, coaching is never directive. The client is always in the driver's seat.

Our teenagers are complete as they are. They do not need us to direct them. They simply want us to enlighten their awareness of the options that are available to them. Teachers must be aware when they are using non-directive, open-ended questions that lead the student to discover their own options for the future.

Parenting, on the other hand, traditionally uses a slightly different approach. As parents, we are taught to direct our children with the main objective being to keep them safe and help them stay on the path most travelled. It is also important to normalize that without our direction, children may not physically survive.

Does this mean that parents should continue to parent with a directive and dictative approach? I think not. I believe that as our children begin to understand and show evidence of developing the skills to communicate, we can include a non-directive parenting approach alongside a 'safety-driven' directive approach when required. I always tell parents that choosing their parenting model should be like choosing the right tool in the toolbox. We would never use a hammer to unscrew anything, now would we? As with a toolbox, we can choose our suitable communication strategies depending on the needs of our children.

SUMMARY OF IF NOT NOW, WHEN?

✓ Reflect on the differences between your career education and the potential for a much more evolved approach with teens today.

✓ Spend time pondering the question: 'What would you do differently if you would have had career guidance and support when you were younger?'

✓ Normalize the realities of what parents want for their children and how teenagers are digesting their wants as fear-mongering expectations.

✓ Surround your students and clients with role models from as many industries as possible. The value of a human conversation with these guest speakers is priceless.

✓ Change the dialogue from a direct dictatorship to an open and growth-minded conversation.

Final Farewell

Parenting, educating, and raising children is not as simple as we hoped it would be. What I have seen in my profession and in my home with my own children is that as our children grow older, our conversations need to be different. Although we cannot always make the sun shine, this does not mean that their future has to feel so bleak.

I want to see more students walk into my office and ask for career discovery support before they make any final decisions about their university destinations. Let us change the direction from 'What university should I go to and what course should I study?' to 'I love building things, so what courses can offer me a career doing just that?' and 'Is university the next step or would vocational study be more effective for me in the next stage of my life?'

With the working world changing at a fast pace and technology evolving even faster, we must prepare our children to fish for their own food instead of waiting for the food to be delivered. Empowerment starts with asking, 'What can I do for the world?', not 'What will the world offer me?'

Acknowledgements

They say that books come through you and this book was certainly an example of that. The idea suddenly came one day and within the next seven months, it was officially created. I must thank Adam Kuestermann for asking me the right question at the right time and for proving to me that the right question really can change your life.

This book both deeply supports my great passion for empowering young adults and ensuring that the conversations about empowerment continue for young teenagers like my students and my children. This work is very personal for me. It is my greatest aspiration to inspire individuals to be motivated and resilient members of society who become role models of character in our community and beyond. I want to thank my students, my clients, and my colleagues for helping me along my path of career enrichment. Without their support, my words could not have been expressed.

I'm profoundly grateful to my children, Dania, Aya, and Sami, for reminding me that parenting is a deeply emotional experience. At the core of our conversations, the messages that have been written in this book are evidence that the future is brighter because our children are becoming more aware and conscious of their purpose and potential.

In writing this book, I remembered my younger years as a teenager. I would like to thank my parents, Filomena and Evangelos Vitoratos, for parenting me during the toughest years of my life. I strongly believe that the learnings I have gained as a coach were possible because of the memories that we shared together all those years ago.

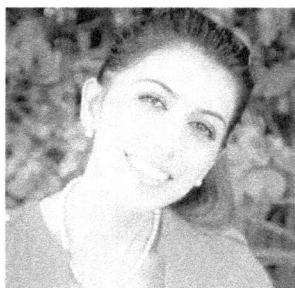

Maria Vitoratos is a life coach, teacher, and mentor who specializes in teen empowerment. She has contributed to the growth and success of individuals, adolescents, and teams over the past ten years. She continues to strive for her personal best in all elements of her career and her life. Her greatest strength is 'moving things forward' while demonstrating commitment to her own professional development, as well as the professional development of her team, her students, and her clients.

Maria is presently leading a Careers Coaching Program with high school students in the United Arab Emirates. Through her work, she is significantly impacting the capacity to influence and manage change within the community. She is passionate about securing the best outcomes for the students in her care and she is determined to energize the team, students, and community in the UAE and abroad.

Maria is a proven leader in her field and the brainchild behind many initiatives that support teenage empowerment, adult development, and the merging of both worlds to inspire a future generation that allows young adults to thrive and reach their full potential.